Lorikeet's Family Surprise
Second Edition

Rainbow Lorikeets are so full of life, their fun-loving, mischievous nature is captivating.

This story, the tenth in the Lorikeet's Book Series for young readers, is based on Larry and Princess Rose returning to the garden with a surprise family.

Through my words and the creative vision of Lillian Falzon, whose illustrations brought these characters to life, I hope you enjoy a peek into the adventures of this quirky, colourful family.

The newly united Rainbow Lorikeets, Larry and Princess Rose, happily fly around with each other, darting in and out of the trees just as they did with their brothers and sisters when they were chicks.

They are always together, whether they are eating, flying or perched in a tree preening one another.

Once they settle on a branch, Larry leans over and rubs his head against Princess Rose, ruffles up her light green collar with his red beak and whispers to her.

Princess Rose lifts her head high and spreads her green cloak to show everyone in the garden how happy and proud she is to have Larry as her lifelong partner.

Their parents, King Royce, Queen Rosanna, Lawrence and Loretta look on remembering what it was like when they too fell in love.

Since Larry and Princess Rose have become a couple, they often go to the garden where the resident human provides sunflower seeds.

When their favourite food of fruit and blossom is plentiful in the trees, Larry, Princess Rose and the Rainbow Lorikeet families don't always visit the garden as the seeds are just a treat and not their main diet.

Larry's sisters, Laura and Lorna, notice that Larry and
Princess Rose have not been to the garden for many weeks.

They ask the other Lorikeets if they have seen them.

The other Lorikeets tell them they had not seen them but
were not worried, Larry loves to find adventure away from
the flock, always coming back with exciting stories.

Larry and Princess Rose have been making house, a cosy home in an old tree hollow.

The nest is lined with dry grass, hair and bark. Princess Rose is sitting on three eggs she laid in the nest to keep them at the right temperature until they hatch.

Larry is on guard, taking his responsibility seriously and only leaves the nest to get food or to scare off unwanted visitors.

It's a happy day for everyone when Larry and Princess Rose return to garden.

They fly in, darting up and down and in-between the trees showing off their colourful coats and flying expertise.

Larry is out in front with Princess Rose following closely behind, leading the three new additions to their family.

Leonard, Lioness and Roxy try their best to keep up with their parents, it is difficult for them not to bump into branches as they awkwardly fly past.

Larry and Princess Rose finally land on a branch high in a tree. Lioness, trying to slow down, manages to cling on to the branch but is hanging upside down.

Leonard completely misses the branch and flies past, bumping into a tree next to them. Roxy flies into her mother, almost knocking her off the branch.

Princess Rose manages to cling on, regain her balance and save Roxy from falling.

All the Lorikeets in the garden gather around to offer their congratulations.

Larry and Princess Rose proudly stand tall, puff out their red and yellow chests and thank everyone for their kind words.

Leonard, Lioness and Roxy, not used to all the exercise and attention have snuggled up together and have fallen asleep under the safety of Larry and Princess Rose' wings.

King Royce, Queen Rosanna, Lawrence and Loretta are in the background, perched in a tree close by.

While patting one another on the back, proudly looking on, they know they have succeeded in bringing up their chicks to be mature, responsible Lorikeets.

Lorikeet's Family Surprise

ISBN

978-1-7642196-9-3 (Paperback)

978-1-7642197-0-9 (eBook)

Website: www.jan-hill-books.com

www.ingramcontent.com/pod-product-compliance
Lightning Source LLC
Chambersburg PA
CBHW060841270326
41933CB00002B/165